LAUGH
-Out-
LOUD
A+
JOKES
for KIDS

LAUGH -Out- LOUD

A+

JOKES for KIDS

ROB ELLIOTT

SCHOLASTIC INC.

ISBN 978-1-338-58670-1

Text copyright © 2018 by Robert E. Teigen. All rights reserved. Published by Scholastic Inc., 557 Broadway, New York, NY 10012, by arrangement with HarperCollins Children's Books, a division of HarperCollins Publishers. SCHOLASTIC and associated logos are trademarks and/or registered trademarks of Scholastic Inc.

12 11 10 9 8 7 6 5 4 3   19 20 21 22 23 24

Printed in the U.S.A.   40

First Scholastic printing, September 2019

Illustrations by Shutterstock/MicroOne, Shutterstock/robuart, Shutterstock/Sudowoodo, and Shutterstock/PinkPueblo.

To all the teachers who work tirelessly to give our kids a wonderful learning experience. Whether you teach in a public or private school or as a home educator, your sacrifice for the next generation is changing the world.

"Teach the children so it will not be necessary to teach the adults."

—Abraham Lincoln

Q: When are teachers like cheese?

A: When they are grating.

Q: How are bus drivers like trees?

A: They both have routes.

Q: What is the funniest time of the school day?

A: Laughter-noon.

Q: What do you need to bring to music class?

A: A note-book.

Q: What do you call the worm that ate Beethoven?

A: A de-composer.

Q: Why did the chemistry teacher stop telling jokes?

A: She never got a reaction.

Student: Does the library have any newspapers or magazines?

Teacher: Periodically!

Q: Why should you give your teacher a comb if he's bald?

A: He'll never part with it!

Q: Why should you tell jokes in anatomy class?

A: The teacher thinks they're humerus.

Knock, knock.

Who's there?

Omelet.

Omelet who?

Omelet smarter than I look!

- -

Cassie: Do you like your astronomy class?

Kelly: It's out of this world!

Annie: I hear you got good grades in cosmetology school.

Lucy: Yes, I nailed it!

Q: What do dogs wear to science class?

A: Lab coats.

Q: Why can't you tell a lie in math class?

A: The teacher knows when your story doesn't add up.

4

Teacher: What can you tell me about the country of Greece?

Billy: It's slippery!

Q: What do whales eat for an after-school snack?

A: Ships and salsa.

Q: What's a pirate's favorite subject?

A: Arrr-ithmetic.

Q: What's something you can catch but not throw in gym class?

A: A cold.

Q: How do the basketball players stay cool during games?

A: They sit by their fans.

Q: What is the best way to get straight As in school?

A: Use a ruler.

Q: Why did the textbook go to the hospital?

A: It needed its appendix taken out.

Q: Why are teachers so awesome?

A: They have a lot of class.

Q: Why did the library book go to the chiropractor?

A: It needed its spine adjusted.

Q: Why don't the cafeteria cooks use spices in the food?

A: They don't have thyme for that.

Q: Why are clarinet players so smart?

A: Because they reed a lot!

Carter: I want to have a space-themed birthday party.

Mom: Great, I'll planet!

Teacher: Are you sure the atom lost an electron?

Student: Yes, I'm positive!

Q: What should you do if your chemistry teacher passes away?

A: Barium.

Teacher: How many sides does a circle have?

Student: I don't know.

Teacher: Never mind, it's pointless!

Teacher: Do you like your book about gravity?

Student: Yes, I can't put it down!

Q: Why were the goats sent to the principal's office?

A: They kept butting heads.

Q: Why did the chicken run onto the soccer field?

A: Because the ref called fowl.

Q: Why don't bumblebees drink coffee before they go to school?

A: They get too buzzed!

Q: What do groundhogs like to read?

A: Pop-up books.

Q: Why did the librarian wear sparkly purple glasses?

A: She wanted to make a spectacle of herself.

Sam: Did you hear the principal wants to marry the school bell?

Joe: Yes, he gave it a ring!

Q: Where do they make all the books for school?

A: In a fact-ory.

Q: Why was the nose feeling sad at school?

A: It kept getting picked on.

Q: What do sea turtles like to study?

A: Current events.

Q: Why did the student throw the calendar out the window?

A: To make the days fly by.

Teacher: Why did you plant your math book in the ground?

Student: So it will grow square roots!

Knock, knock.

Who's there?

Spell.

Spell who?

W-H-O!

Q: What do teachers drink in the winter?

A: Hot chalk-olate.

Q: Why did the lobster get a time-out at school?

A: It was being shellfish.

Q: Why did the farmer study geometry?

A: He already had a pro-tractor!

Student: What can you hear but never touch or see?

Teacher: Your voice.

Q: Why did the thermometer go back to college?

A: It wanted another degree.

Knock, knock.

Who's there?

Zinc.

Zinc who?

Zinc you will pass the chemistry test?

Q: Where do science teachers eat their lunch?

A: At the periodic table.

Knock, knock.

Who's there?

Water.

Water who?

Water you making for the science fair?

Q: Why can't you take your hamster to school?

A: They don't make backpacks that small.

Q: What is the difference between a kid and a fish?

A: One has Cs in school, and the other has a school in the sea.

Q: Why did the English teacher buy a rocking chair?

A: So she could sit for a spell.

Q: Why did the gym class learn karate?

A: The teacher thought they would get a kick out of it!

Q: Why did the math teacher have a nervous breakdown?

A: He had too many problems to solve.

Q: Why did the whale need a cello?

A: So it could join the orca-stra.

Q: Why didn't Jenny go to the library?

A: She was already booked!

Q: Why couldn't Jake join the track team?

A: There were too many hurdles.

Q: What does your music teacher need when it rains?

A: A hum-brella.

Q: What do rabbits play at recess?

A: Hop-scotch.

Q: What is the smartest state in America?

A: Alabama, because it has four As and a B.

Q: Why don't they serve rabbit in the cafeteria?

A: Kids don't like hare in their food!

Q: Why does Sally bark every morning when she gets to school?

A: She's the teacher's pet.

Q: When is it stinky at school?

A: When the cafeteria lady is cutting

the cheese.

Q: Where do cows eat their lunch at

school?

A: In the calf-eteria.

Q: What do science teachers

eat after dinner?

A: Experi-mints!

Q: Why did the girl bring a ladder to school?

A: She wanted a higher education.

Q: When is an English teacher like a judge?

A: When she hands out sentences!

Q: Why did the teacher have to turn out the lights?

A: Because her students were so bright!

Teacher: Jill, why did you miss class yesterday?

Jill: I didn't miss it! But I was sick.

Q: What is the difference between a teacher and a train?

A: A teacher makes you spit out your gum, while a train says "chew, chew, chew."

Q: Why was the clock looking forward to spring break?

A: It needed to unwind.

Q: What did the buffalo say to his child when he left for school?

A: Bi-son.

Q: Why did the penguin skip its first day of school?

A: It got cold feet!

Teacher: Can you give me an example of an interrogative sentence?

Jenny: Do I have to?

Teacher: Well done!

Q: Why did the hogs drop out of school?

A: Because they were boar-ed in class.

Teacher: How did Benjamin Franklin feel when he discovered electricity?

Student: He was shocked!

Q: When do students take their umbrellas to class?

A: When they're brainstorming.

Q: What do you call it when the cafeteria burns the meat?

A: A mis-steak.

Q: What happened when the magician failed his classes?

A: He pulled out his hare.

Knock, knock.

Who's there?

Donut.

Donut who?

Donut worry. I'm sure you'll pass your test!

Teacher: What should you do about a rash from biting insects?

Student: Don't bite them in the first place!

- -

Knock, knock.

Who's there?

Jamaica.

Jamaica who?

Jamaica good grade on your report card?

Q: Why did the toad get sent to the principal's office?

A: It was a bully-frog!

Q: What do you get when an elephant runs through the cafeteria?

A: Squash!

Knock, knock.

Who's there?

Needle.

Needle who?

Needle little help getting your homework done?

Knock, knock.

Who's there?

Honeybee.

Honeybee who?

Honeybee a dear and sharpen my pencil.

Knock, knock.

Who's there?

Broken pencil.

Broken pencil who?

Never mind, there's no point!

Q: What do you do when your dog eats your English paper?

A: Take the words right out of his mouth!

Knock, knock.

Who's there?

Orange.

Orange who?

Orange you glad we don't have school tomorrow?

Q: Who is in charge of all the school supplies?

A: The ruler.

Q: Why did the kid carry a dictionary in his pocket?

A: He wanted to be a smarty-pants!

Q: Why did the computer stay home from school?

A: It had a virus.

Q: Why did the computer teacher scream?

A: She saw a mouse.

Q: What is a math teacher's favorite dessert?

A: Pi.

Q: What did the slug say when he got an A on his paper?

A: I snailed it!

Q: Why did the kid put his protractor in the refrigerator?

A: Because it was 180 degrees!

Q: Why was the chicken late for school?

A: She didn't hear the alarm cluck.

Joe: Why do you always cry at lunchtime?

Bill: Because we're in the cafe-tear-ia!

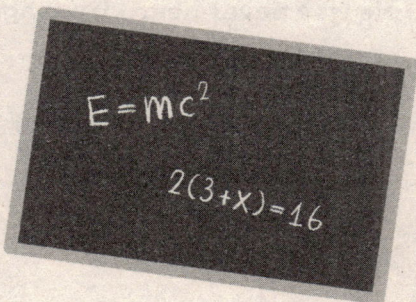

$$E = mc^2$$

$$2(3 + x) = 16$$

Q: What do you get when you take a picture of a plant?

A: Photo-synthesis.

Amy: Did you hear about the atoms who were dating?

Annie: Yes, but I heard they just split!

Leah: Did you hear about the kid who studied to be a mime?

Emma: No, what happened?

Leah: He was never heard from again.

Q: What does a cow pack in its lunch box?

A: Peanut udder and jelly sandwiches.

Knock, knock.

Who's there?

Gnome.

Gnome who?

I gnome I'm going to fail the pop quiz.

Q: What do you drink if you're thirsty in dance class?

A: Tap water.

Q: Why did the monkey get detention?

A: He was a bad-boon.

Q: Why did the Skittles go to school?

A: They wanted to become Smarties!

Teacher: Why can't a nose be twelve inches long?

Student: Because then it would be a foot!

Knock, knock.

Who's there?

Polka.

Polka who?

Polka me one more time, and I'll tell the teacher!

Q: Why did the science teacher throw his chair?

A: He was a mad scientist!

Q: Why did the whale get detention?

A: He was chewing blubber gum in class.

Q: What happened when the janitor slipped on the wet floor?

A: He kicked the bucket!

Q: What happened when the library flooded?

A: It caused a title wave.

Q: What do fish use for their lunch money?

A: Current-cy.

Q: Why did the corn on the cob pay attention in class?

A: It was all ears.

Q: Why did the band teacher bring jelly to class?

A: He wanted to have a jam session.

Q: Why was the triangle good at basketball?

A: It always made three pointers.

Q: What do English teachers eat for breakfast?

A: Synonym rolls.

Q: Why did the teacher send the window to the principal's office?

A: It was being a pane!

Q: **Why can't frogs get college degrees?**

A: They croak before they finish.

Q: **Why can't elephants join the swim team?**

A: They're always dropping their trunks!

Q: **Why was the art teacher famous?**

A: He was good at drawing crowds.

Q: **What is a witch's favorite subject in school?**

A: Spelling.

Q: Why did the kid fail his survival skills test?

A: It was too in-tents.

Teacher: Which is faster, hot or cold?

Student: Hot! It's so easy to catch a cold.

Knock, knock.

Who's there?

I am.

I am who?

You don't know who you are?

Q: What happened when the teacher colored her hair purple?

A: She dyed!

Teacher: Why were you late for class?

Student: I was attacked by a tissue on the way to school.

Teacher: How did you get away?

Student: I kicked the snot out of it!

Q: What happened when the ghost cheated on his homework?

A: The teacher saw right through him.

Teacher: Why is England such a wet country?

Student: It has a queen who's reigning.

Knock, knock.

Who's there?

Sticker.

Sticker who?

Sticker backpack in your locker and go to class!

Q: How did King Arthur finish his education?

A: He went to knight school.

- -

Q: Why was the broom late to school?

A: It over-swept.

Knock, knock.

Who's there?

Iran.

Iran who?

Iran to catch the school bus, but I

missed it!

Knock, knock.

Who's there?

Mustache.

Mustache who?

I mustache the teacher a question

about the test.

Q: Why wouldn't the two 4s go out for dinner?

A: Because they already "8."

Q: Why did the student wear a shower cap to school?

A: He didn't want to get brainwashed.

Q: Why did the kid wear a life jacket to school?

A: The teacher said he was on thin ice!

Q: Why did the horse go to the guidance counselor?

A: It wasn't feeling very stable.

Knock, knock.

Who's there?

Ketchup.

Ketchup who?

Ketchup or you'll be late for school!

Q: Why didn't the moon eat all of its lunch?

A: Because it was full.

Q: What do you get when you're bored in art class?

A: Cra-yawns.

Q: What kind of dogs do they let into the library?

A: Hush puppies.

Q: What is a boa constrictor's favorite subject?

A: World hissss-tory.

Knock, knock.

Who's there?

Elsie.

Elsie who?

Elsie you after school.

Mom: How was your day, son?

Son: I got in trouble with the teacher for
something I didn't do.

Mom: Oh no, what was it?

Son: My homework.

**Q: Why did the boy take a prune to
the prom?**

A: Because he couldn't find a date!

Knock, knock.

Who's there?

Disgusting.

Disgusting who?

**Disgusting wind is blowing my papers
all over.**

Q: How did the cows get to school?

A: On a com-moo-ter train.

Q: Why did the orange fall asleep in class?

A: It ran out of juice.

Q: Why do oranges always finish their homework?

A: They know how to concentrate.

Q: Why did the almond report to the principal's office?

A: It was going nuts!

Q: Why don't rivers ever run out of lunch money?

A: They're always by the banks.

Q: How did the bull pay for his lunch?

A: He charged it!

Q: What do you call a school on a mountain?

A: A high school!

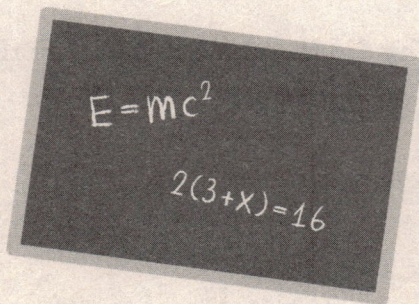

Q: Why did the kids get stung at school?

A: There was a spelling bee.

Q: Why did the car have excellent handwriting?

A: He had fine motor skills.

Q: Why did the wasp get sent to detention?

A: It wouldn't beehive in class.

Q: Why wouldn't the skeleton try to learn at school?

A: It was a numbskull!

Q: Why did the book join the FBI?

A: It wanted to go undercover.

Q: What did the art teacher say when he was arrested?

A: I didn't do it—I was framed!

Q: What kind of snake is good at math?

A: A pi-thon.

Student: I thought of a joke about sodium and hydrogen.

Teacher: Would you like to share it with the class?

Student: NaH.

Q: Why aren't trees good at taking tests?

A: They're always stumped!

Q: What kind of bugs are good at math?

A: Account-ants.

Q: How did the brontosaurus feel after soccer practice?

A: Dino-sore.

Q: Why did the frog join the track team?

A: It was good at tadpole-vaulting.

Q: What kind of dog is never late to school?

A: A watch-dog.

Q: Why do the marching band members have such clean teeth?

A: They always have a tuba toothpaste.

Knock, knock.

Who's there?

Sherwood.

Sherwood who?

Sherwood be nice if I passed this test!

Q: Why is your guitar teacher so stressed out?

A: She's always fretting!

Q: Why did the teacher fall in love with her boots?

A: She said they were sole-mates.

Teacher: Who can tell me the capital of Washington?

Student: W.

- -

Q: Why did the chicken join the marching band?

A: It already had two drumsticks.

Q: What does a clam wear to gym class?

A: A mussel shirt.

Knock, knock.

Who's there?

Razor.

Razor who?

Razor hand in class, please!

Knock, knock.

Who's there?

To.

To who?

Don't you mean "to whom"?

Q: Why did Humpty-Dumpty sign up for gym class?

A: He needed the eggs-ercise.

Knock, knock.

Who's there?

Pasture.

Pasture who?

It's pasture bedtime and you have school tomorrow!

Knock, knock.

Who's there?

Funnel.

Funnel who?

Funnel start when the school bell rings for recess.

Q: Where does the music teacher keep his sandwich?

A: In his lunch Bachs.

Teacher: What has four eyes but can't see?

Student: Mississippi.

Q: What do you call a bull that sleeps in class?

A: A bulldozer.

Teacher: How do we know carrots are good for our eyes?

Student: I've never seen a rabbit wearing glasses!

Teacher: What do you call the past, present, and future?

Student: I'm not sure, but it sounds tense!

Teacher: What travels around the world but stays in one place?

Student: A stamp.

Q: What is a kid's favorite day of the week?

A: Fri-yay!

Teacher: Who can tell me the capital of Alaska?

Student: Don't Juneau?

Q: Why did the students take off their shoes in class?

A: The teacher said to put footnotes in their papers.

Q: Why didn't anyone use the skunk's ideas for the science project?

A: Because they stunk!

Knock, knock.

Who's there?

Anita.

Anita who?

Anita get my grades up or I'll be in trouble.

Knock, knock.

Who's there?

Iowa.

Iowa who?

Iowa lot of lunch money to the cafeteria.

Q: Why did the boy get kicked out of band?

A: He was always in treble.

Q: Why did the tree keep going to the school nurse?

A: It was a sycamore.

Teacher: What kind of snake comes out after it rains?

Student: A rain-boa.

Q: Why did the guitar hate going to band practice?

A: It was always getting picked on!

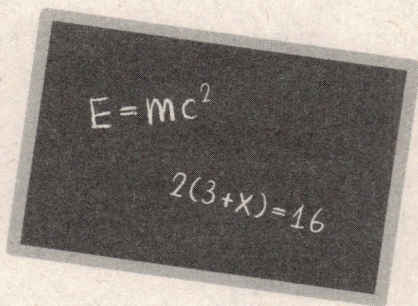

$$E = mc^2$$

$$2(3 + x) = 16$$

Knock, knock.

Who's there?

Alaska.

Alaska who?

Alaska student and see if he knows the answer.

Q: What did the United States say to France at midnight?

A: Europe too late and you have school tomorrow!

Q: Why don't kids in the choir get good grades?

A: They only go for the high Cs.

Knock, knock.

Who's there?

Window.

Window who?

Window we get another break from school?

Knock, knock.

Who's there?

Twain.

Twain who?

Twain hard and you can join the soccer team.

- -

Knock, knock.

Who's there?

Quiche.

Quiche who?

**Quiche your mom before you leave
for school!**

Knock, knock.

Who's there?

Joe King.

Joe King who?

**Joe King too much will get you sent to
the principal's office!**

Q: What is the worst kind of candy?

A: Homework assign-mints!

Q: What is a whale's favorite thing to do on the playground?

A: The sea-saw.

Q: Why was the cow so popular?

A: Because it was adora-bull.

Q: What do art teachers drink with their breakfast?

A: Crayon-berry juice.

Q: Why did the tree get sent to the principal's office?

A: It was a knotty pine!

Q: Why did the cow believe everything the students said?

A: Because it was so gulli-bull!

Q: Why did the kid want to study only sharks?

A: He was a fin-atic!

Q: What time is it when an elephant sits at your desk?

A: Time to get a new desk!

Teacher: What is your favorite letter?

Student: Y.

Teacher: Because I want to know.

Student: Y.

Teacher: Go to the principal's office!

Q: How do smart students get to college?

A: On scholar-ships!

Teacher: How many antelope live in Africa?

Student: A gazelle-ion!

- -

Q: How do clams call their parents after school?

A: They use their shell phones.

Knock, knock.

Who's there?

Avenue.

Avenue who?

Avenue taken this spelling test before?

Q: What is an astronaut's favorite part of the school day?

A: Launch time!

Q: **Where does a bee wait for a ride?**

A: At the buzz stop.

Q: **What did George Washington call his false teeth?**

A: Presi-dentures.

Q: **Why did the dog get expelled?**

A: It was a pit bully!

Q: **Why are math teachers hard to get along with?**

A: They create a lot of division!

Q: **How are flowers like the letter A?**

A: Bees come after them.

Teacher: What starts with an E and ends with an E and has only one letter in it?

Student: An envelope!

Q: Why couldn't the cat go on the field trip?

A: It didn't have a purr-mission slip.

Knock, knock.

Who's there?

Watson.

Watson who?

Watson the cafeteria menu today?

Q: Why do astronomy teachers eat lunch by themselves?

A: They need a lot of space.

Knock, knock.

Who's there?

Oscar.

Oscar who?

Oscar if she knows the answer to the math problem.

Q: How do birds fasten their gym shoes?

A: With Vel-crow.

Q: Why was the teacher drinking Coke in class?

A: She wanted to have a pop quiz.

Q: What do you call a cat that wants to be a nurse?

A: A first aid kit-ten.

Q: How does an acrobat celebrate the end of the school year?

A: He does summer-saults!

Q: What do you give a dog who does extra homework?

A: Bone-us points!

Q: Why was the sailor upset over his report card?

A: His grades were at C level.

Q: Why is it so hard to get along with chemistry teachers?

A: They're always over-reacting!

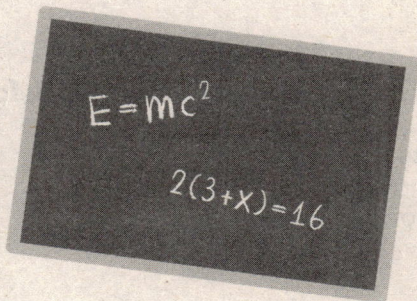

$$E = mc^2$$

$$2(3+x) = 16$$

Knock, knock.

Who's there?

Icy.

Icy who?

Icy you got an A on your test!

Q: Why did the beaver cross the playground?

A: To get to the otter slide.

Q: What happened to the frog before its final exams?

A: It got worry warts!

Knock, knock.

Who's there?

Izzy.

Izzy who?

Izzy going to try out for the football team?

Knock, knock.

Who's there?

Ada.

Ada who?

Ada big breakfast today before school!

Knock, knock.

Who's there?

Handsome.

Handsome who?

Handsome pencils over so I can take this test.

Knock, knock.

Who's there?

Itchy.

Itchy who?

Bless you! Do you need a tissue?

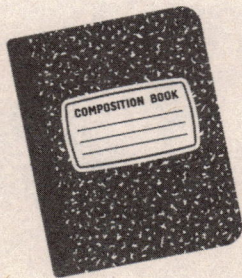

Knock, knock.

Who's there?

Hayden.

Hayden who?

Hayden seek is fun to play at recess!

Q: What kind of shoes do mice wear to gym class?

A: Squeakers.

Q: Why did the bee have to go to the school nurse?

A: It was breaking out in hives.

Knock, knock.

Who's there?

Honeydew.

Honeydew who?

Honeydew you know it's time for school?

Q: Why did the jellyfish always get picked on at school?

A: It was spineless.

Q: What did the paper say to the pen?

A: Write on!

Q: What do sharks like to play at recess?

A: Swallow the leader!

Q: Why did the apple go to gym class?

A: So it could work on its core.

Knock, knock.

Who's there?

Leaf.

Leaf who?

Leaf your books in your desk for tomorrow.

Q: **What happened when the pig became a writer?**

A: It used a pen name.

Q: **Why did the snail stay home from school?**

A: It was feeling a bit sluggish!

Knock, knock.

Who's there?

House.

House who?

House it going at school these days?

Student: Do you want to hear my joke about germs?

Teacher: No!

Student: Why not?

Teacher: Because I don't want it to spread!

Knock, knock.

Who's there?

Canoe.

Canoe who?

Canoe help me with my homework?

Q: Why did the boy bring his piggy bank to football practice?

A: He wanted to be a quarter-back!

Q: Why did the beaver study astronomy?

A: It wanted to go to otter space.

Knock, knock.

Who's there?

Gladys.

Gladys who?

Gladys time to go home for the day!

Q: Why did the clock get detention?

A: It was tocking too much in class.

Q: How do crocodiles do their math homework?

A: They use a calcu-gator.

Q: Why did the princess go to school?

A: To find her prince-ipal.

Q: What's a frog's favorite kind of music?

A: Hip-hop.

Knock, knock.

Who's there?

Sara.

Sara who?

Sara snow day tomorrow?

Knock, knock.

Who's there?

Russian.

Russian who?

I'm Russian to get to school on time!

Knock, knock.

Who's there?

Anita.

Anita who?

Anita dollar for hot lunch!

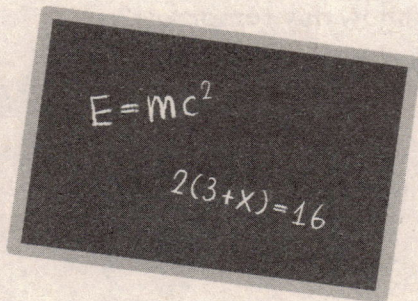

$$E = mc^2$$
$$2(3+x) = 16$$

Knock, knock.

Who's there?

Abbott.

Abbott who?

Abbott time you finished all your homework!

Knock, knock.

Who's there?

Yukon.

Yukon who?

Yukon go to the library after school!

Knock, knock.

Who's there?

Pecan.

Pecan who?

Pecan someone your own size!

Knock, knock.

Who's there?

Theodore.

Theodore who?

Theodore is jammed, and I can't get into the classroom!

- -

Knock, knock.

Who's there?

Hugo.

Hugo who?

**Hugo to the principal if you don't
behave!**

**Q: Why don't chickens like gym
class?**

A: They think it's eggs-hausting!

**Q: What do you get when you bring
your fishing pole to the library?**

A: You get a bookworm!

Knock, knock.

Who's there?

S'more.

S'more who?

There s'more jokes where that came from!

Charlie: Have you ever seen a catfish?

Jerry: Yes, but I don't think he caught anything.

Q: What do you get if there are mosquitoes in the computer lab?

A: Mega-bytes!

Q: Why did the gorilla get in trouble at school?

A: It was going bananas!

Q: Why did the pig drop out of school to get a job?

A: It wanted to bring home the bacon.

Q: What do you put in your lunch box for a field trip in the desert?

A: Sand-wiches.

Q: What do cows do on the first day after Christmas break?

A: Make their moo year's resolutions.

- -

Q: Why did they serve hay in the cafeteria?

A: A kid said he could eat like a horse!

Q: How did they know who stole paint from the art room?

A: They caught the thief red-handed!

Q: Why did the poodle stay home from school?

A: It was sick as a dog.

Q: How do bugs feel about summer vacation?

A: Exuber-ant!

Teacher: What's your report about?

Student: My new underwear.

Teacher: Well, keep it brief!

Q: Where do plants go to college?

A: Ivy League schools!

Teacher: In what month do kids cheat on their tests?

Student: Fib-ruary!

Q: Why did the early bird need a ruler?

A: It wanted to catch an inchworm.

Knock, knock.

Who's there?

Sawyer.

Sawyer who?

Sawyer bus at the bus stop.

Q: What goes tick, tick, woof, woof?

A: A watch-dog.

Q: Why did the astronaut work in the cafeteria?

A: Her food was out of this world!

Q: Why was the porcupine always late to school?

A: It was a slowpoke.

Q: What did they give the top student in dental school?

A: A plaque!

Tim: I hope they serve fish in the cafeteria.

Mark: I'm sure they will if the fish brings lunch money.

Q: What do dogs bring to class on their birthdays?

A: Pup-cakes.

Q: Why did the fish drop out of school?

A: It was floundering.

Q: What happened to the mole when it got bad grades?

A: It was grounded.

Knock, knock.

Who's there?

Ethan.

Ethan who?

Ethan teachers need a summer vacation!

Knock, knock.

Who's there?

Lucas.

Lucas who?

Lucas time to tell another joke!

Q: How much did the wasp pay for its school supplies?

A: Nothing. It got free-bees.

- -

Q: Where did the sick peach nap at the nurse's office?

A: In an apri-cot.

Q: What did the horse put in its lunch box?

A: Straw-berries.

Q: Why did the firefly need an after-school snack?

A: It had a light lunch.

Q: In the classroom, where do frogs sit?

A: On toadstools!

Q: What is the school band's favorite month?

A: March!

Knock, knock.

Who's there?

Abby.

Abby who?

Abby stung me on the playground!

Q: When is a race car like an honors student?

A: When they're accelerated!

Q: Why do librarians move so fast?

A: They have to book it!

Q: What do you call a cow with a telescope?

A: A star-grazer.

Q: What does a crocodile drink after gym class?

A: Gator-ade.

Q: What did the class clown eat for lunch?

A: A peanut butter and jolly sandwich.

Q: What happened to the dog when it swallowed the teacher's watch?

A: It got ticks.

Q: What's the band teacher's favorite movie?

A: *Beauty and the Beats*.

Q: How do you make a bandstand?

A: Take away their chairs.

Q: What does the music teacher take to bed with him every night?

A: His sheet music.

Knock, knock.

Who's there?

Pencil.

Pencil who?

Your pencil fall down if you don't wear a belt.

Q: What happens if you play hide-and-seek with an elephant on the playground?

A: You win every time!

Q: How did the moon feel after lunch?

A: Full!

Knock, knock.

Who's there?

Amish.

Amish who?

Amish school during summer break!

Q: What do you call a school dance in the winter?

A: A snow-ball.

Knock, knock.

Who's there?

Rita.

Rita who?

Rita good book lately?

Q: What's the coldest letter in the alphabet?

A: Iced T.

Q: What do you call a teacher with a tissue?

A: The boogie-man!

Knock, knock.

Who's there?

Atlas.

Atlas who?

Atlas it's time for the weekend!

Q: What did the psychology book say to the math book?

A: Tell me about your problems.

Q: What happened when the witch cheated on her test?

A: She was ex-spelled.

Q: Which animal won't write its name on its homework?

A: Anony-moose.

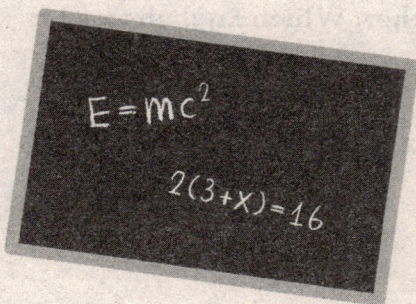

Q: When do you need headphones in science class?

A: When your experiment is radioactive.

Q: Which is your lightest textbook?

A: Your gram-mar book.

Q: What do sailors like to read?

A: Ferry tales.

Teacher: Which English word is always misunderstood?

Student: Misunderstood!

Q: What do you call a kid with no lunch money?

A: Nickel-less.

Q: Why did the cheerleader bring her dog to school?

A: For the pup rally!

Q: Why did the tree take a nap after school?

A: It was bushed.

Q: What do airplanes and football players have in common?

A: They both have touchdowns.

Jenny: Did you hear that grandparents are invited to school today?

Josie: That's old news!

Knock, knock.

Who's there?

Oliver.

Oliver who?

Oliver pencils need sharpening.

Q: Why did Mary's little lamb follow her to school?

A: It heard school was woolly fun.

Q: How did the swim team get to school?

A: They carpooled.

Knock, knock.

Who's there?

Washington.

Washington who?

I'm Washington of dishes in the cafeteria.

Q: What do chickens play in the orchestra?

A: Bach, Bach, Bach.

Q: How do you catch your music teacher?

A: With a clari-net.

Q: What happened when the teacher ran out of glue?

A: It was a sticky situation.

Q: What do you get when you cross Shakespeare and honey?

A: To bee or not to bee, that is the question.

Knock, knock.

Who's there?

Iguana.

Iguana who?

Iguana juice box in my lunch today.

Q: Why can't you sell joke books at school?

A: Your teacher doesn't want any funny business.

Sam: Did you hear the school nurse lost the scale?

Tom: No weigh!

Knock, knock.

Who's there?

Brooke.

Brooke who?

Brooke it to class before you're late!

Teacher: I finally found my watch.

Student: It's about time!

Emma: Are you allowed to write a book?

Anna: Yes, I'm author-ized.

Q: Why did they have to clean up the court after the basketball game?

A: All the players were dribbling.

Knock, knock.

Who's there?

Peas.

Peas who?

Peas hand in your homework.

Q: Why did the pig stay home from school?

A: It had the swine flu!

Q: Why did the bee go to see the school nurse?

A: It was getting hives.

- -

Q: Why did the pig always get in trouble in class?

A: Because he was such a ham!

Knock. Knock.

Who's there?

Irish.

Irish who?

Irish I could take the test over!

Knock, knock.

Who's there?

Snow.

Snow who?

Snow much love for my classes!

Q: What kind of animal always falls asleep in class?

A: A dino-snore.

Knock, knock.

Who's there?

Weed.

Weed who?

Weed better get a snow day tomorrow!

- -

Knock, knock.

Who's there?

Dewey.

Dewey who?

Dewey have to take the test today?

Knock, knock.

Who's there?

Emma.

Emma who?

Emma long way away from the end of the school year!

Knock, knock.

Who's there?

Riley.

Riley who?

Riley hope I passed the test this time!

Knock, knock.

Who's there?

Melon.

Melon who?

My teacher is one in a melon!

Q: Why did the tiger get suspended?

A: It was always lion.

Q: Why can't you trust a rubber band?

A: It's always stretching the truth!

Q: Why did the choir teacher bring a goldfish to class?

A: So the kids could practice their scales.

Q: What kind of snack did they serve in computer class?

A: Computer chips.

Knock, knock.

Who's there?

Owen.

Owen who?

Owen my teacher a couple missing assignments!

Q: Why was the teacher sad when she found out she had Dracula in her class?

A: Because she heard he was a pain in the neck!

Q: Why do fish always argue with their teachers?

A: Because they like to de-bait!

Q: Why did the bike not want to drive home after school?

A: Because it was two tired!

Q: How did the orange cut in the lunch line?

A: It squeezed its way in!

Knock, knock.

Who's there?

Raymond.

Raymond who?

Raymond me to bring my library book to school tomorrow.

Knock, knock.

Who's there?

Bear.

Bear who?

Bear with me while I try to figure out this homework.

Knock, knock.

Who's there?

Lava.

Lava who?

I lava school, but I lava summer break more!

ROB ELLIOTT

is the bestselling author of *Laugh-Out-Loud Jokes for Kids, Knock-Knock Jokes for Kids, Laugh-Out-Loud Animal Jokes for Kids, More Laugh-Out-Loud Jokes for Kids, Laugh-Out-Loud Doodles for Kids, Laugh-Out-Loud Spooky Jokes for Kids, Laugh-Out-Loud Christmas Jokes for Kids, Laugh-Out-Loud Awesome Jokes for Kids,* and *Laugh-Out-Loud Road Trip Jokes for Kids*. His popular joke books have sold more than 3.5 million copies. Rob has been a publishing professional for more than twenty years. He lives in West Michigan, where in his spare time he enjoys laughing out loud with his wife and five children.